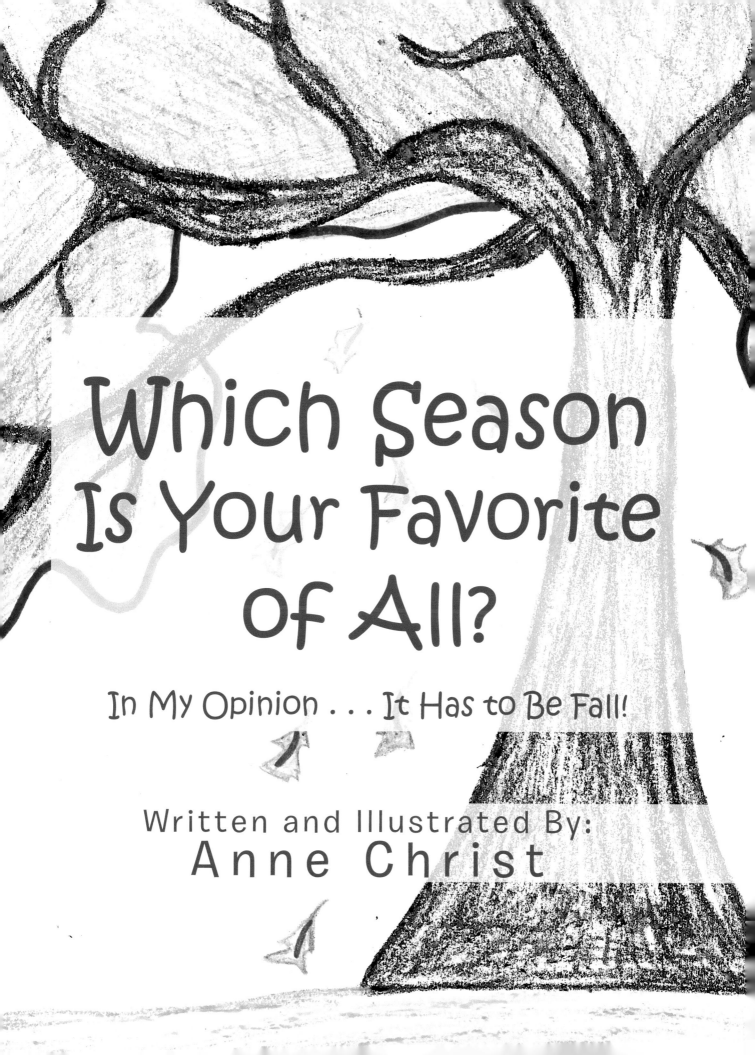

Which Season Is Your Favorite of All?

In My Opinion . . . It Has to Be Fall!

Written and Illustrated By:
Anne Christ

To order additional copies of this book, contact:
Xlibris
1-888-795-4274
www.Xlibris.com
Orders@Xlibris.com

Which Season Is Your Favorite Of All?

In My Opinion . . .
It Has to Be Fall!

For Jackson, Jacob, John
Walker, and Annsley Noelle
DREAM BIG!

March is the time when birds love to sing;
They call to each other and announce, "It is **Spring**!"

The deer run in the meadow and leap up and down,
So graceful and swift, they don't make a sound.

The rabbits come out of burrows in the ground,
They listen to the birds while on top of their mound.

Beavers are happily swimming in their streams,
Collecting up sticks and working as teams.

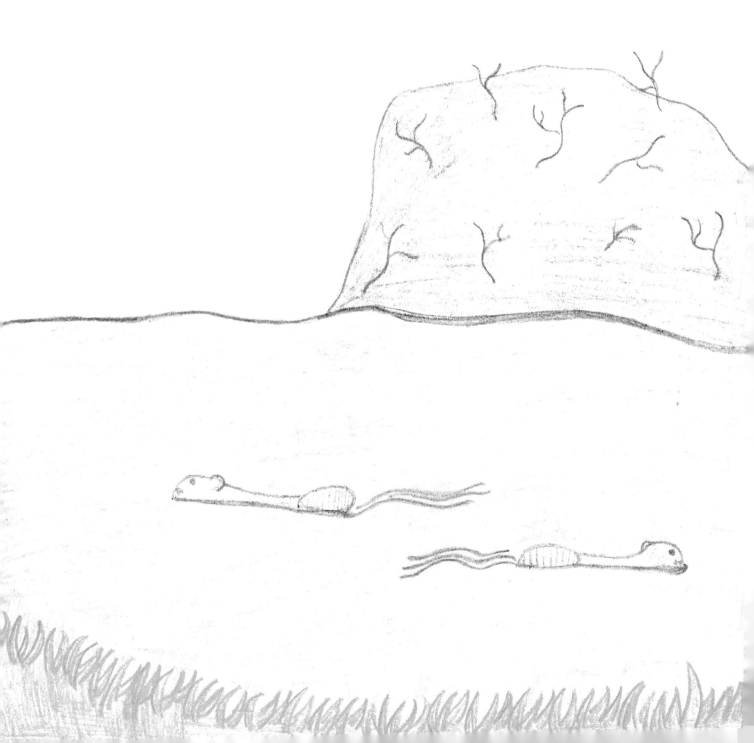

Trout start to jump and bears start to feast,
The fish don't even know to fear this big beast.

Frogs start to jump and then start to croak,
Making funny noises deep down in their throats.

The animals are excited because warm weather is near
All animals come out like there is nothing to fear.

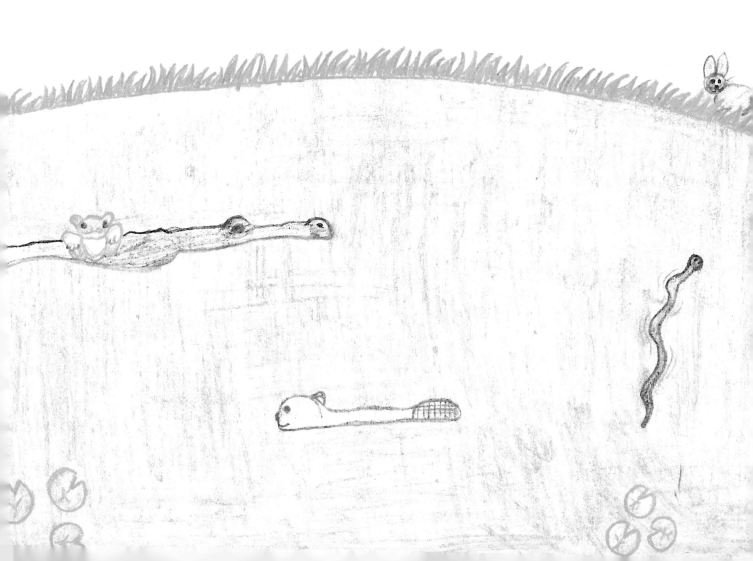

Everyone is happy and getting along...
And all of this started with one bird and his song!

Spring is long gone and
Summer is finally here,
All animals will awaken with the
footsteps that draw near.

The night animals go home and sleep during the day,
It is too hot for these animals to come out and play.

Crickets start to chirp when the sun starts to show,
Its big orange face that radiates a glow.

It gets so very hot; so animals will come to play,
At their favorite water holes at the end of the day.

They come to the edge and look in the lake,
And can see their reflections and the funny faces they make.

Birds say their, "Good Mornings," but don't stay for long,
It even gets too hot for the birds to sing a sweet song.

Squirrels play in the shade and keep as cool as they can,
Today a cool breeze serves as a fan.

Soon the hot turns to cool as **Fall** draws near,
All the animals become more active because they love
this time of year!

Can you guess the most beautiful season of all? Well in my opinion.....It has to be **Fall**!

The leaves on the trees turn yellow, orange, and red
Then they start to fall.....all around your head.

They fall into big piles and children love to play
In these big soft piles until the end of the day.

The animals gather food for the long winter ahead,
They know snow will come soon and they need a winter bed.

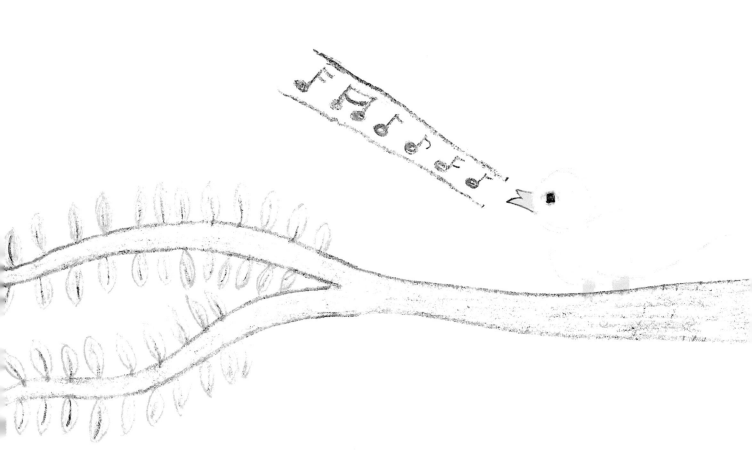

Most animals fatten up so they can sleep all winter long,
They won't come back out to play until they hear the
birds **Spring** song.

Temperatures start to change and nights will start to get cold,
It's a warning to animals to find shelter from an upcoming
Winter that will be bold

Halloween is in the **Fall** and kids go trick or treat
And fill their little bellies with all the candy they can eat.

So button up your coat and pull up
your boot
Because before too long, you won't
even hear an owl hoot!

We have learned that **Fall** is cooler weather
and everyone comes out to play....
Such a beautiful season, and the children
play all day!

Winter

Winter is a cold time when snow starts to fall,
And all of the animals hibernate in a neat little ball.

They sleep for several days while the world outside turns white,
The snow on the ground so beautiful and bright.

Most of the animals stay put in their den,
Along with their kind, their family, and kin.

It's a long, hard winter but the bears sleep right through,
The dream of **Spring** and all they will do.

When **Spring** is getting close, the groundhog comes out,
And everyone watches to see if **Spring** is in route.

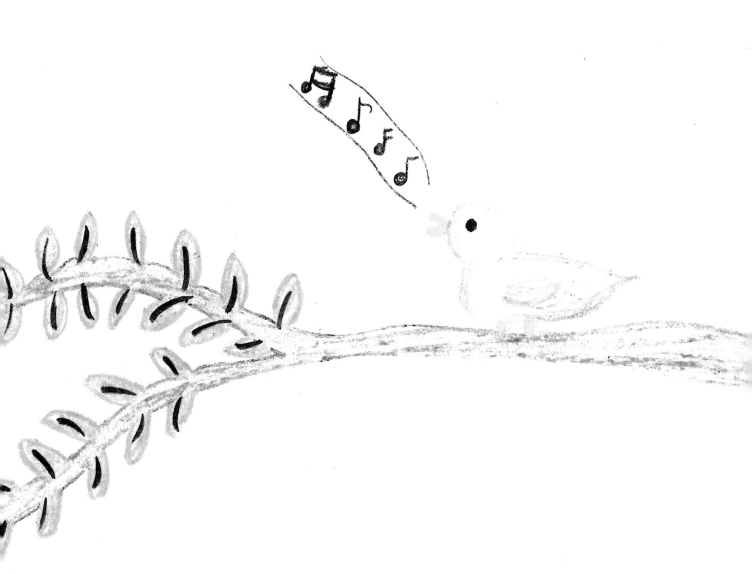

Because if he sees his shadow, then **Spring** is drawing near;
And the birds will come out and their **Spring** song....we will hear.

Snowflakes are beautiful and fall with such grace,
The deer look around and it covers their face.

So **Winter** is cold, but families snuggle up tight,
They get rested for **Spring** and its beautiful sight.

Printed in the United States
By Bookmasters